The People's History

Ferryhill
and District

by

Anne Dixon

A rare and wonderful photograph of Mr William Henry Barron seen here tending to his livestock of many varieties at his smallholding in Dean Bank, Ferryhill *circa* 1940.

Previous page: A typical underground scene showing a Putter at work in the bowels of Dean and Chapter Colliery sometime in the 1950s. The Putter's best friend was his pony which was used to haul coal or supplies in a tub (a small truck which held 15-20cwts) constituted of wood or steel.

Copyright © Anne Dixon 2001

First published in 2001 by

The People's History Ltd
Suite 1
Byron House
Seaham Grange Business Park
Seaham
Co. Durham
SR7 0PY

ISBN 1 902527 25 9

Contents

Ferryhill Village postmarked 1906. The Town Hall was built upon the site of the old poor houses in 1867. The garden occupies the site of the original St Luke's Church (designed by Ignatius Bonomi of Durham) which was built in 1829. Ferryhill became a parish in its own right in 1843. The first St Luke's Church was demolished and some of the stone incorporated in the new St Luke's Church which was completed by 1853 (I presume that since the land on which the first St Luke's was built would still be consecrated ground it would be considered more fitting to have a garden there rather than a secular building such as a Town Hall!). The pond survived for several years after the building of the Town Hall and the laying out of the garden.

This book is dedicated by Anne Dixon in memory of her husband Tom Dixon, her Father and Mother Jack and Myra Kitching and also in memory of her Father and Mother-in-law Tom and Terry Dixon, who appear in the photographs.

Introduction

When asked to compile a book on Ferryhill and the villages around from my collection of old photographs and postcards, I was excited at the opportunity. I knew that this would be a great challenge but very enjoyable. I have included a selection of photographs hoping they will all help to provide a valuable record of Ferryhill and District in the past and be of interest to present and future generations. My main interest some eight years ago, when I started collecting, was what the village and village life were like in the days of our forefathers. The heritage of Ferryhill and the surrounding area, for hundreds of years was rooted in agriculture and mining. This situation changed with the arrival of the railways around 1840. Access to large markets by rail resulted in new, larger and deeper mines being sunk: Leasingthorne 1842, Little Chilton (Bull Crag) 1852, Broom 1870, Chilton 1872, East Howle 1873, Mainsforth 1876, Windlestone 1876. Whilst the owners of these mines provided local housing for their workforce, there was a small number of miners who travelled from Ferryhill Village to work in these mines. The sinking of Dean and Chapter Colliery on the northern edge of the village in 1902-1904, changed this situation dramatically. The colliery was the largest and most modern in the area. At its peak over 2,600 men and boys were employed producing over 750,000 tons of coal per annum. To house the workforce and their families, Dean Bank, consisting of some 1,000 houses, was built by the Bolckow Vaughan and Co Coal Company between 1902 and 1907. As a result, the population of the village increased from 3,123 in 1902 to 10,674 by 1921. Most of the houses in the old village of Ferryhill were built of stone and were lit by paraffin lamps, then later gas was installed. Coal fires were used to heat the houses and on washing day a set pot boiler was used to boil all white garments and towels with a posstub and stick to beat the clothes clean and a large tub and mangle to remove all surplus water. Families did a lot of walking, some of the regular walks were down Doggy Wood and over the fields to Cornforth or to Ferryhill Station. Other popular walks were Strawberry Lane and Bankie Fields and to Hett and East Howle. To the South a favourite walk was by way of the bunny banks and on to Chilton.

A lot of children and adult entertainment was centred around the many churches and chapels in the area. There were concerts, anniversaries and

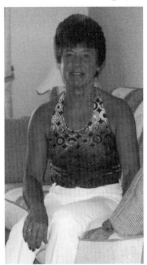

activities such as the making of silver paper pictures, board games and reading classes. All village children played various games, sometimes in groups or in twos and threes in someone's yard or around the village square. Girls played with dolls and prams or took part in various skipping games which were very popular as were various ball games, hitchy dabbers, tally-oh, tiggy and hide and seek. Boys played marbles, ran miles with hurley and crook, rode horses, played football, cricket, rounders, knock-on-nine-doors with the girls (the girls usually got caught) and tying two door knobs together then knocking on both doors and running off to watch from a safe distance.

In this volume of The People's History we look back at Ferryhill and District, its people and their work and play, and history and development throughout the last 150 years. May you, the reader, find this volume as fascinating and rewarding as I have in compiling it.

Acknowledgements

The author appreciates the valuable help given by many people in the preparation of this book; many of them are residents of the villages I have covered who, over the past few months, have kindly loaned me photographs and postcards. Without their help this book would not have been possible. If I have used your photographs and inadvertently have not acknowledged your kindness, my apologies and thanks.

Beamish Hall Photographic Archives, Sedgefield Borough Council, Ferryhill Parish Council, North of England Newspapers, Mr Denham, Dean Bank School, Doris Predki, Mr J. Hepplewhite, Cleves Cross School, Marjorie Hebdon, Mrs Mary Wilkinson, Mr Dick Sewell, Kevin McCartin, Marion McCartin, Tommy McCartin, John and Betty Hope, Peter and Margaret White, Joan Shearer, Barry Richardson, Irene Holt, Ruth Charlton, Mr & Mrs J. Cross, Derek and Valerie Cartwright, Mr & Mrs Paul Holmes, Mrs Nora Robinson, Tracey Fenwick, Mrs Sandra Fenwick, Alec & Joyce Morland, Vince and Pauline Carr, Mrs Nellie McCormick, Geoff McManners, Martin Farlow, Ernie Saunders, Jack Best, Mrs Anita Kirkup, Mr & Mrs Lidster, Mr & Mrs Fodden, John Allinson, Joe Ward, Norman and Isabelle Dunn, Mr David Blair, Mr Robin Walker, Mr John Matthews, Carol Allaker, Peter and Jean Collins, Bob and Freda Welsh, Mrs Gladys Turnbull, Ada Stephenson, George Bruce, Wally and Joy Anderson, Mrs Hilda Wright, Pam Greathead, Arthur Bulman, Pauline Land, Mrs Ashett, Dorothy Ashett, Debra Eggleston, Nicola Eggleston, Gordon Harris, Mr D. Whitfield, Mr W. Davison, Mr P. Kerrison, Mrs Barker (née Adamson), Mr L. Eltringham, Mr & Mrs K Kisby, Mr Graham Snaith, Mrs Mary Hall, Mr Billy Curry, Ann McKenna, Dean McKenna, Joe Kendall and Mrs Cynthia Rothwell.

I should also like to thank the following who are sadly no longer with us, for their readiness to help: Mr Alderson, Joan Williams, Mr George Charlton and Mr Bill Fairless.

Special thanks to Andrew Clark of The People's History for his help and guidance, Mr George Nairn for supplying photographs and cards from his collection, Mr Frank Bellwood for providing photographs and allowing me to make use of his research on Mainsforth Village, Mrs Margaret Hayes for typing my notes and finally Miss Alice Thompson for photographs, information, proof reading my notes and her enthusiasm and support.

STREETS AND BUILDINGS

FERRYHILL VILLAGE. Nº 568.

Ferryhill Village – one of the oldest postcards in my collection, date unknown, shows the original stone construction of the Town Hall centre with North Street on the left. Several of the buildings shown have been demolished in the last 70 years and replaced with others such as the library and the residential home. Market Street on the right has been altered much over the years. Most of the premises are now shops. Note the hand water pump on the right and the poor state of both the path and the road.

FERRYHILL: THE ABANDONED ROAD-WORKS.

This interesting illustration from 'The Great North Road' by C.G. Harper (published 1901) shows the old A1 as it was in August 1900, winding down the hill from Ferryhill Village on its way northwards to Durham. Clearly seen in the distance is the Ferryhill 'Cut' with two of its bridges and Ferryhill Village to the left silhouetted against the sky. The large building to the right in the foreground is the Brewery. The abandoned earthworks on the left have a sorry tale to tell.

Before the Trustees of the Boroughbridge and Durham Turnpike road determined in the early 1830s to begin improvements to this section of the Great North Road, travellers from the south and from the north had to climb the limestone escarpment and skirt the edge of the old village of Ferryhill. The route up the hill from the north would be particularly hard work for the horses drawing coaches or heavily laden carts, while the descent of the steep hill must have been 'hair-raising' for the passengers, in winter especially. The road to the north led down the hill to the very bottom of the valley (just below Red Hall Farm).

Once the decision had been made, the Turnpike Trust began quarrying out vast quantities of limestone from the escarpment to the west of the village to form a by-pass and filling in the valley to the north with rock and soil in order that those coaches and other horse drawn vehicles not requiring to stop at the village could pass more speedily and directly on their way. When the new road reached Ferryhill Bankfoot, ie the bottom of the hill, the Trust built a bridge across at the point where the Clarence Railway Company was driving through the Byers Green Branch line to carry coal eastwards to Hartlepool. It was at this point that the road works came to a halt as a result of a dispute with the Clarence Railway Company over repairs to the new embankment damaged by the railworks. The Byers Green Branch Railway continued to carry coals but work on the new road would not be resumed until after the 1914-1919 war. Finally in 1923 the road was officially opened and the first vehicles drove triumphantly through.

These two historic photographs, looking south, show work in progress on the Ferryhill road diversion around 1921, still with much work to do. The bridge in the foreground was used by the miners to gain access to Dean and Chapter Colliery from the village. The centre bridge leads to the Dean Bank (housing developed to accommodate the influx of miners to the new colliery), while the iron footbridge gives access to the store houses built

by the Bishop Auckland Co-operative Society. The second photograph, taken on the south side of the footbridge, shows the new road on the south side of the Cut with West Street on the left. The gentleman on the extreme left is Mr Will Gamsby, road foreman.

Ferryhill Market Square, showing the Town Hall with the War Memorial in the gardens. The building on the immediate left was Wearmouth's Farm. The site is now occupied by Feryemount Residential Home. The foundation stone was laid by the Rt Honourable Harold Wilson, OBE MP on 17th July 1970.

This monument (now sadly minus the obelisk) which stands in the garden in front of the Town Hall is a tribute to William Walton (overman) who sacrificed his life rescuing two boys at Dean Bank, 8th August 1906. Erected by the officials and workmen of Dean and Chapter colliery.

Ferryhill Village *circa* 1936. The view shows market day and also on the right foreground, Burrells the newsagent. Although there have been a number of alterations over the years, it is believed that this shop (throughout the 20th century) remained a newsagent. Today it is owned by I & V Harper. To the right can be seen J & W Tate, general dealers – now the location of the North Eastern Co-operative supermarket.

The Greyhound Inn, Market Street, Ferryhill Village *circa* 1930s is one of the village's long established public houses and still in business today. It is possible that the landlord Arthur A. Winter is the gentleman with rolled up shirt sleeves standing in the doorway.

Market Street, Ferryhill Village *circa* 1900. This view shows part of a garden (later tarmaced over) created on the site of the former village pond. Note the large building on the right, with very attractive chimney stacks. It is thought that it had been a butchers' shop since it was built until 1993 when Mr John Allison, the last butcher to occupy these premises, moved nearer to the centre of the village. It is now a factory outlet owned by Mrs Lynne Robinson.

MARKET PLACE, FERRYHILL

Market Place, Ferryhill 1935. The Post Boy on the left has remained externally largely unchanged over the years. In 1908 it was a low two storey building with a pantiled roof and the main entrance from the main road at the top of Durham Bank.

East side of Ferryhill, looking towards Manor Farm *circa* 1936 with the Manor House on the right. The large building on the left is the Masonic Lodge. This was a building owned by Pallisters who sold it to the Rowlandson Lodge of Freemasons in the mid 1920s. It was altered to suit the needs of the members and dedicated on 31st August 1927. To the left is the old Village Church School built in 1847 and enlarged in 1870 to accommodate 250 pupils at a cost of £577. Note the horse-drawn cart tied to the barrier in front of the School House and the water pump on the right hand side of the road. Hand water pumps were installed around the village and water was carried to the homes usually in enamel pails.

The Manor House Ferryhill, 1980. Steeped in history it is probably one of the oldest buildings in Ferryhill, built late 1600s/early 1700s and restored in 1891. It stands on the south side of the village, an ancient and picturesque building. Above the doorway in

one of the walls of the garden is a stone bearing the inscription.

Sic Siti Laetantur Lares

'How happily seated those lares are who feed on prospect and fresh air
dine moderately every day
and walk their supper time away'

Church Lane, Ferryhill, from a card postmarked 1924 clearly showing the bell tower of St Luke's Parish Church. On the left is the Gaiety Picture House which since closing as a cinema in the early 1960s has been used as a ballroom, a dance hall, a bingo hall and a gymnastic centre. The building was demolished in 1994.

A fine photograph taken outside the entrance to the Gaiety Theatre (demolished in the last few years) in the Back Lane, now Church Lane, Ferryhill just before or at the beginning of the 1914-1918 war with what are believed to be theatre staff and possibly a group of artistes playing at the theatre that week. The manager of the theatre in 1914 is known to have been Frederick P. Varley – he is perhaps one of the two tall gentlemen standing under the glass canopy which is decorated in the Art Nouveau style.

Darlington Road, Ferryhill, looking North, dates from the early 1900s and shows well established tradesmen such as Gallons Ltd (grocers) Meadow Dairy (provisions dealer) and Williams (watch repairer and jeweller). Many of the shop fronts have changed over the years as have the businesses. Note the lack of a footpath down the left side of the road and the old gas light. Visible in the distance is the Black Bull Hotel.

Another photograph of Darlington Road, Ferryhill early 1900s. This time the local children pose for the camera. Note the girls are wearing button up boots and the boys laced boots and black stockings.

Darlington Road, Ferryhill looking South on what appears to be a winter's day *circa* 1900/1910. Everyone seems to be waiting for something. A fine milk churn sits upon its cart and a horse toils up the hill pulling its load.

The West End of the village *circa* 1930 with the Bay Horse on the extreme left. Blue House Farm in the centre distance at the top of Parker Terrace (where West End Post Office is today) was farmed by Fosters. It was a stopping place for changing horses on long journeys. The large bay window of the Black Bull Inn can be seen on the far right, then Roberts (men's drapery), Todds (wet fish and vegetables), Herbert Brown (tobacconist, confectioner and barber), Walter Wilson (general dealer) and Wells (fruit and vegetables).

Durham Bank, Ferryhill *circa* 1930. The Saddlers Arms in the foreground was owned by Vaux, the landlord at that time being J.T. Clelland. The gable end of the Kings Head Hotel can be seen further up the road. The road to the right led down the bank to Dean and Chapter Colliery.

On 19th May 1906, Bishop Auckland Co-operative Society opened a branch store in Dean Bank, Ferryhill. It was a corrugated iron, single storey building which was to supply the miners of Dean and Chapter Colliery and their families with provisions for several years. When the brick built, two storey Co-op replaced it several years later, the original shop became the premises of Blamire Printers until well into the second half of the 20th Century.

This view of Eldon Terrace shows the Ferryhill Station branch of the Bishop Auckland Co-operative Society which was formally opened on 4th June 1904 by Mr John Rogerson, the esteemed Manager at Spennymoor. A monster tea was held on the occasion and as the day was

beautiful and fine, the members from all quarters flocked to the event and the new hall was tested to its utmost capacity. About 500 people were regaled with the cheering cup and a most successful concert followed the tea and ended a day which will long be remembered a red letter day in the locality. The Ferryhill Branch opened under the most auspicious circumstances and has since rendered good service to the community and the Society. The photograph was taken prior to the building of Croft Gardens on the opposite side of the road. The building now houses the Home Lighting Specialists since 1970.

Watt Street *circa* 1910. These houses were constructed for Dean and Chapter mineworkers and their families by the Coal Company between 1902 and 1907.

This postcard dated 1904 shows Deanhurst almost ready, apart from a few final touches, for the manager of the new Dean and Chapter Colliery to take up residence. The colliery was sunk between 1902-1904. After the closure of the colliery in the late 1960s the house was sold to John Dee (John Dee International Transport Company). Finally in the 1980s the property changed hands again, becoming the Denehurst Nursing Home and with the subtle change in the spelling of the name the connection with the Dean and Chapter of Durham, the original owners of the land upon which the house stands, was finally severed.

Main Road, Dean Bank, Ferryhill looking West *circa* 1910. On the left is Dean Bank School built in 1907. On the right from the front you have Ferryhill Baptist Church, the Police Station, the Cinema, Miners' Welfare Hall and Reading Room followed by St Cuthbert's Terrace.

Westcott Terrace, Dean Bank, Ferryhill from a postcard marked 1909. The scene and buildings have changed very little. As can be seen, traffic was not a major problem in those days, just one horse drawn cart on the road. Note the walled and railed front gardens. The iron railing were removed to make ammunition during the 1939-1945 War.

Owen Street, Dean Bank 1907. On Saturday 16th February 1907, Thomas Ellwood moved into No 4 Owen Street (4th house from the right) from Mainsforth Rows with his wife Alice and children Jane, Ralph, Lillian and Alice. At that time he was earning  from £2/£3 per week (pay day was once a fortnight!) With the help of a loan from his father-in-law and his own savings, Thomas bought the house which cost £257, a great amount of money. The workmen look as if they are in the process of surfacing the road. Iron railings were in due course fixed to the low walls in front of the houses. At the beginning of the 1939–45 War, those iron railings were removed to be smelted down and used in the manufacture of armaments. Behind the unseen photographer stands Dean Bank Council School.

Broom Road, Ferryhill early 1900s. The scene and buildings have changed very little. Osborne Terrace on the left had several shops including Marleys (butcher) Bulmans (newsagent), Grahams (post office) – thought to have been run by two sisters – Dot White Drapers and several more. Now most of them are private residences. The street on the right is Rowlandson Terrace at the top of which was Jones the Dentist.

The Great North Road (now the A167) at Thinford pictured here in 1955. The former Dean and Chapter Colliery pit heap, now landscaped, can be seen in the background to the right.

East Howle – interesting to see villages that have gone. These rare photographs
of East Howle were taken in the 1950s and are the only photographs so far
discovered which show the rear of Pit and Railway Streets. They are probably
the last photographs taken before the streets were demolished between 1960 –
1970. Note they still have the coal house doors, but the midden hatches have
been removed and bricked up. I wonder how many people remember using
them. Coal houses and netties are relics from the past.

An early photograph of Ferryhill Station taken *circa* 1870 showing the Eldon Arms Hotel dominating the scene. That area of land to the immediate left of the wire railings was used as part of the Cattle Market for penning animals ready to be transported by rail in the days before the cattle waggons came into being. The Royal Mail Sorting Office has yet to be erected; this came in 1895 when the project was undertaken by local builder George Lazenby's company. Both Eldon Terrace and Croft Gardens have also to be erected on the left of the picture. The building centre right with a prominent bow in its roof, which is thought to have been thatched, was demolished by 1905 and stood as a vacant plot until the Durham Miners' Association commissioned George Lazenby in 1927 to erect the Miners' Welfare Institute, known to locals at the 'tute'. The miners of Mainsforth Colliery paid a few coppers each week from their wages towards the building and its upkeep. Once the hub of social activities for the miners and their families, the Welfare Hall was noted throughout the County, especially during the Second World War years when couples travelled for many a mile to enjoy the Saturday night dance where they could dance to some of the best dance bands of the time. Many will also remember the brilliant performances of Mainsforth Operatic Society who played to a packed audience night after night with a quality of entertainment that was unbeatable. The building is presently run by Mainsforth and District Community Association and is still used by local groups, including the Operatic Society.

Inside Mainsforth Welfare Hall on the day of the Queen's Coronation, 2nd June 1953.

Mainsforth Colliery Welfare Institute. The building contractor was Lazenby. The Welfare Institute has been a centre of social activity and a focal point for many celebrations for the miners and their families. Mainsforth Colliery no longer exists but the Welfare Institute, now Mainsforth Community Centre, still serves the people of Ferryhill Station.

Chilton Lane, Ferryhill Station. The row of miner's cottages which once stood on the right were demolished a considerable number of years ago. The large building on the slope was once a chapel. After its closure it was used by a local business for storage. As the result of a fire it was so badly damaged that it was finally demolished.

Chilton Lane, Ferryhill Station, *circa* 1904, taken from a card postmarked 20th September 1907, clearly showing the church and the church hall of St Oswald. Behind the church stands Ferryhill Station School, built in 1878 and still serving the needs of the district. When the church was demolished, St Oswald's church bell was presented to the school by the Rev Michael Snowball, Vicar of St Aidan's Church, Chilton in March 1989. Note the poor state of the road.

Chilton Lane, Ferryhill Station. The old stone built cottages on the right were demolished a number of years ago. The shops on the left are now private residences.

Looking South along Darlington/Durham Road, Chilton. This view shows the original shop fronts, many of which have now changed, on a rather quiet day *circa* 1930-35.

Windlestone Cottages, Rushyford *circa* 1900. Clearly seen are the estate houses roofed with clay pantiles, a form of roofing which was quite common then, but few examples of which remain today.

Windlestone Hall *circa* 1900, a mansion of ashlar stone with a colonnade of Doric pillars at the front.

These excellent photographs show beautifully laid out gardens around Windlestone Hall *circa* 1900.

The Hall was the seat of the Eden family for over 100 years and birthplace of the former Prime Minister, the late Sir Anthony Eden. It was built for Sir Robert Johnson Eden, Bart, about the year 1830 on the site of a former manor house. The cost, including the handsomely laid out grounds in which it stood, was at the time a staggering sum of £40,000.

This wintery picture at Rushyford *circa* 1900 shows a group of children trudging down through the snow from school at the top of the hill. The school has since been converted into a house. The cottages you see were home to the Windlestone Hall estate workers until the great sale of 1936. The second cottage from the left is known to have been the smallest post office in Great Britain. It closed in 1989, having been run for 39 years by Jane Aldred, who had taken over in 1950 from her mother, Isabella Hunter, who had run it since 1900.

Not a lot is known about this photograph other than that it is at Leasingthorne, outside the Eden Arms Hotel, *circa* 1920. What the occasion is I do not know.

Kirk Merrington South View on the left, with Ramshaw Terrace, Coronation Terrace and Jowsey Place on the right *circa* 1900.

A postcard of Hopkinson Place, Kirk Merrington taken by photographer Mr H. Coates of 70 High Street, Willington, Co Durham. The dress of the children suggests that it probably was taken *circa* 1900. Note the horse and trap.

A well known shop in Front Street, Kirk Merrington was that of H. Valks, grocer and draper. It has been a general dealers and the village post office for a number of years. Since 1983 it has been owned and run by Frances and George Brown.

The village of Kirk Merrington although small had no fewer than six public houses: the Greyhound, the Half Moon, the Fox and Hounds, the Three Horse Shoes, the White Hart and the Bay Horse. Of the six, three no longer exist. The White Hart was demolished and the site is now occupied by private dwellings. The Bay Horse was converted into a private house and only recently the Three Horse Shoes has ceased to continue as a public house. In this very early photograph can be clearly seen the Fox and Hounds centre with the Half Moon on the left and on the right the sign hanging over the door of the Three Horse Shoes. Quite visible on the right are two horse drawn carts standing outside the village smithy *circa* 1900.

A group of locals assembled outside of the 'Ship Inn', Middlestone Village *circa* 1920s.

Middlestone Village probably early 1900. Not a vehicle in sight, so quiet and peaceful. This photograph, which shows the Ship Inn on the extreme left, is very rare. Not many photographs of this village have survived and there is little information about it. Note in the distance the imposing square tower of the Church of St John at Kirk Merrington.

PEOPLE

Thomas Edward Ellwood, his wife Alice and their two oldest children Jane Ann (Jenny) and Ralph pose for this fine studio portrait about 1903. Thomas began work as a deputy at Mainsforth Colliery on Wednesday 30th August 1906 but moved from Mainsforth Rows to 4 Owen Street, Dean Bank on Saturday 16th February 1907 just after the street had been completed. A self taught exponent of DIY – as were so many miners and working men – Thomas would stick at nothing, doing his own house repairs, shoe and clock repairs and mat making. He built a lean-to greenhouse onto the back of the house, where he grew tomatoes and chrysanthemums and rented a large council allotment, growing vegetables and a variety of flowers. He kept active and busy in his garden until a couple of years before his death in 1955 at the age of 81.

Mrs Sarah Pratt (better known as Granny Pratt by the folk of Ferryhill) with her husband and family *circa* 1900. Granny Pratt was a well known local trader whose sweet shop was located on Main Street, Ferryhill. She was a familiar figure with her horse and trap at the local markets. When she died at the age of 93 within a few weeks of her 94th birthday, she had been a widow for 30 years and left five sons, whose ages ranged from 64 to 73, three sons having died. There were also 34 grandchildren, 52 great-grandchildren and 3 great-great-grandchildren!

On Tuesday 12th July 1921, the funeral carriage of Dr James Linn Shirlaw, drawn by a pair of gleaming black, well groomed horses passes the Methodist Chapel at the East end of Market Square. A popular and well respected man, Dr Shirlaw was noted for his caring and kindly manner, a quality shared by many village doctors of the early 20th Century. The cortege was preceded by a guard of honour formed by the local constabulary, who were followed by members of Ferryhill Rowlandson Lodge of Freemasons, Brethren from other Lodges, family and friends. The great respect in which Dr Shirlaw was held is obvious from the number of people lining the route.

Harry Wilkinson born 18th May 1920 known as Sergeant Major Wilkinson during his army career. The photograph shows Harry, proudly wearing his medals, standing outside the Town Hall, Ferryhill on Armistice Day 1995. Sadly Harry died 16th September 2000, much loved and respected by the people of Ferryhill who knew him.

Below: 'The Two of Us' – Harry and Mary Wilkinson of Broom Cottages, Ferryhill married 4th July 1942. This studio photograph was taken at Taylors Photographers, Bishop Auckland one year after they were married.

These women are wartime ambulance drivers. Night time driving was very hazardous since the headlights were almost completely blacked out – only a narrow beam was allowed. On the left is Grace Scullion, an accomplished pianist, who had been born in Rangoon, Burma. She came to live in Ferryhill in 1934. Centre is Alice Allanson, who helped her parents run their home based fried fish and chip shop at the bottom of Darlington Road.

During the Second World War all able-bodied civilians were expected to contribute to the war effort. A very important section of Civil Defence was the ARP (Air Raid Precautions) which included Fire Watchers, First Aiders and Ambulance drivers. In Ferryhill, the ARP Post was in the Masonic Hall. When the sirens went you had to stop whatever you were doing, no matter what it might be – you might be fast asleep, you might be in the bath (no time to get dried), you might be cooking a meal – you had to run! Seen here are First Aiders Muriel Rutherford (on the left) and Alice Ellwood.

Ferryhill St John Ambulance Brigade Cadets with their Captain Elizabeth (Lizzie) Binks and Assistant Officer Alice Ellwood, outside the St John Ambulance Brigade Hall, Dean Bank. The cadets usually met once a week to practise First Aid. Back row: Margaret Routledge, Enid Ryan, Elsie Johnson, Nellie Stephenson, Audrey Kell, Anne Haswell and Mary Slater. Middle row: Unknown, unknown, Alice Thompson, Pat Rock, Nellie Maddison and Letty Thompson. Front row: Mary Peaker, Rosemary Leathley, Captain Elizabeth Binks, Asst Officer Alice Ellwood, Nellie Barrass, Pauline French and ? O'Kane.

The Welfare Ground, Dean Bank, Ferryhill was opened in 1926 during the Strike. Seen here is Bob Thompson, believed to have been the first groundsman of Dean Bank Recreation Ground.

This lovely family photograph shows George and Greta Bruce of Westcott Terrace, Dean Bank,Ferryhill with their children Gloria and Ian, sitting on the banks of the River Wear after watching miners from the collieries throughout County Durham carrying their Lodge Banners into Durham City and onto the Race Course on Durham Miners Gala day *circa* 1954.

What a wonderful photograph – dressing up time for Gloria and Ian Bruce inside 18 Westcott Terrace, Dean Bank, Ferryhill. The photograph was taken by their father George Bruce *circa* 1954.

This photograph taken Summer of 1936 shows the fine signpost which once stood at the bottom of Wood Lane, Ferryhill. The small girl is Lettice Thompson with a family friend. Lettice, or Letty as she later insisted on being called, for obvious reasons, was staying on holiday at No 4 Owen Street, Dean Bank with her mother's sister who was housekeeper for Letty's grandfather Thomas Ellwood.

Molly Dunlavey of Ferryhill is quite happy to pose for the photographer in her confirmation dress.

This is definitely one for the family album. Three little girls – probably sisters – pose for J.B. Smithson Photographer, Ferryhill.

This wonderful photograph is of young Joe McCormick standing outside his front door, Ferryhill, *circa* 1920s.

In the front garden of 90 Darlington Road, Ferryhill, in 1941, the McLean family all lined up posing for the camera as they did on many occasions. This picture was taken by their father Mr Harrison McLean who was a keen photographer. From the left are: John (15 years), Mary (13), Doris (12), Alan (10), Nancy (8), Marjorie (6) and Lily (2).

Taken *circa* 1944, the picture shows L.N.&R. Lee drapers, one of the well known shops in Darlington Road, Ferryhill. Staff at the time, left to right: Mrs Willey, her mother-in-law Mrs Willey, Mrs Lee (shop owner) with her assistant Doris McLean. The building is now a branch of Barclays Bank.

An advertisement in St Luke's Church magazine in 1931. The Jones Brothers were in business as cycle agents in Darlington Road, Ferryhill some time before 1929 and the business continued in the hands of one of the brothers until well after the Second World War.

H. Leonard's electrical and hardware shop in Parker Terrace, Ferryhill. Irene Holt, seen here as a young woman with her colleague Harry Thompson, the radio engineer, started working at Leonard's shop when she was 16 years of age and remained there for 48 years until she retired.

The staff at the Meadow Dairy, Darlington Road, Ferryhill 1944-45. At the back is Nellie Davies with Joan Routledge and Audrey Fox in front of her. In the front row are: Renee Myers, Doris Riley and Hilda Cotton. All were Ferryhill girls except Doris Riley who came from Chester-le-Street.

We're having a wonderful time! It's Lily McLean's birthday party at 16 Thirlmere Road, Ferryhill, *circa* 1940. Such a spread! There are ham sandwiches, homemade cakes, jelly, ice cream and for this special occasion Mum's best china cups are being used! Even the dog wants to be part of it all. Lily is the one on the right wearing glasses. Included in the celebrations, left to right are: Nancy McLean, Dorothy Young, Sheila Young, Betty Hodgson, June Gamsby, Carol Shellhorn, Marjorie Shellhorn, Marjorie McLean and Mary Dunn.

Andrew Predki outside Gardners Photographers, 102 Church Lane, Ferryhill, now a private residence. Church Lane was known as Hurford Terrace until May 1952.

All smiles on this lovely picture of families from Ferryhill on one of the many coach tours from the village taking them on an outing, on this occasion to Redcar in the summer of 1950. Among those in the picture are: Lily McLean (Junior), Lily McLean (Senior), Eva Wright, Stan Wright, Phyllis Wright, Annie Carr, Marjorie McLean, Doris McLean, Doris Wright, Alec Wright and Margaret Wright.

Two beautiful examples of Baby's 1st birthday postcards dated 29th April 1917. The cards are addressed to: Miss M.J. Nicholson, 6 Hurford Terrace, Back Lane, Ferryhill. The message on one reads: 'Dear little Mary Jane, this card is to wish you many happy returns of your birthday with lots of love and kisses from S. Jane Fawcett.' Mary Jane Nicholson, well known to the people of Ferryhill as Jennie McCartin sadly died on 1st July 1998.

This well dressed lady, Lena Barron (now Mrs Lena Ashett), 21 years of age poses for the camera in Newton Street, Dean Bank, Ferryhill in 1929.

This delightful photograph shows Joan Williams aged 4 years old, holding on to the hand of her younger brother Stan aged 2 years outside No 6 Faraday Street, Dean Bank, Ferryhill in 1934. Note the slate to the left of the door, on which is chalked the time the miner of the house wanted wakening by the 'knocker up' or 'caller', a man employed by the Coal Company to help get men to work in the early shifts before alarm clocks were in general use. The time on this slate is 2.00 am in the morning. From this we know the miner was on foreshift, which usually started between 2.00 am and 4.00 am.

A beautiful photograph of the Carr family standing outside 73 Rennie Street, Dean Bank, Ferryhill. From left to right: Annie, John and Elizabeth Carr with their mother and grandmother.

Mr William Henry Barron and his granddaughter, Dorothy Ashett, pose for this photograph in the backyard of 66 Bessemer Street, Dean Bank, Ferryhill *circa* 1949.

'Just Good Friends' – Frank Ripley and Dorothy Ashett sitting on the doorstep of 66 Bessemer Street, Dean Bank, Ferryhill *circa* 1949. Note the well worn proddy mat.

Sitting on the doorstep of 18 Carlton Street, Ferryhill Station some time in 1947 is Mr Joseph Stanley Kendall, a coal miner at Mainsforth Colliery, with his son also called Joe, aged 2 years, standing alongside him. This photograph was taken just before Mr Kendall set off to start his shift at the pit.

Who would have thought that Ferryhill Village had its own telephone exchange! Well, here are the photographs to prove it. It was in the front room of Mr & Mrs Hutchinson of 15 Osbourne Terrace, The Broom, Ferryhill *circa* 1944.

Mr Hutchinson, with his wife looking on, connects his caller and from the smile on his face appears to be enjoying the conversation!

Standing outside of 15 Osbourne Terrace: Jean Sewell, Winsome Hutchinson, Mrs Hutchinson, Mr Hutchinson and Miss Jean Angus.

Craftsman Dick Sewell inside the joinery workshop of George Lazenby in the 1950s. Dick started his apprenticeship with the company in 1941 when he was just 14 years of age and after giving 51 years service he retired in 1992.

Photograph of the Lazenby Builders and Haulage ARW (Air Raid Wardens) team seen here in the builders yard, Ferryhill Station *circa* 1943. Back row: George Varley, Stan Stephenson, Kenny Shilson, Arthur Bulman, Hughie Thompson. Middle row: Arthur Bell, Jacky Meek, William Stephenson, George Hilloughby. Front row: Dougie Batson, Dennis Hails and George Hilloughby's young son David.

A group of miners standing outside Ferryhill Station Workmen's Club and Institute, *circa* 1920.

William Holdsworth and his wife Elizabeth were amongst the first couples to occupy one of the 16 Mainsforth Colliery houses built by the Carlton Iron Company for junior officials and a number of key workers. North Terrace was situated approximately 200 yards to the North of the East Pit shaft and screens; the terrace was in an east to west alignment so that the rear of the houses looked out upon the colliery yard. A narrow road fenced off with old railway sleepers divided the yard where, excepting for a narrow strip of grass, the Colliery shops were situated; these included the Welders, Joiners, Fitting Shop, Blacksmiths and Electricians with the offices of the colliery engineer, Mr Tom Peacock and his assistant Engine Wright Mr Bob Armstrong adjoining. An

electrically operated guillotine for cutting and punching steel bars stood outside the Blacksmiths' shop, with an area for laying out work and machinery; this was usually overflowing with gear. A few yards in front of the shops stood the loco repair shed, steel bar racks and sand shed (for loco wheel grip) next the rail sidings that delivered empty waggons under the screens to be filled with coal. At the east end of the screen the plate layers cabin stood at the bottom of a flight of concrete steps that led up the Heapstead. At the left of the steps was the Choppy House where Mr Albert Tyreman, the Head Horse Keeper, was in charge of a number of men who saw to all the needs of both surface and underground ponies The Heapstead was mainly a stock yard for both timber props and steel girders and an area for spare tubs, that were made and repaired at a nearby Tub Repair Shop. Opposite stood the Coal Cutting Repair Shop, with the Pick and Drill Repair Shop next door. Behind stood the sawmill and a hanger, where conveyor chains for underground use were repaired, and finally there was the Pug Mill where concrete was mixed mainly for underground use.

Sadly North Terrace was demolished shortly after the colliery closed in 1968. A list of some of the early tenants follows: Richard and Elizabeth White, William and Elizabeth Holdsworth, James and Jane Ann Barton, Frank and Catherine Jefferson, John and Edith Sayers, James and Mary Jane Garbutt, Ernest Foster and John Henry Wearmouth, William and Alice Fawcett, Arthur and Jennie Robinson, John and Jane Wardle, Alfred Bowron, John and Hannah Colledge also Robert, Thomas and Jane Mawston, Thomas and Jane Prattley. Others remembered include Harry Holt (First Aid Man), Freddy Kirkby and Bob Reed (welders), Jack Jefferson (pipeman), Harry Bowron (carter).

Mainsforth was noted as an extremely well-managed and progressive colliery; this was reflected in the high quality of its officials and of its manpower, particularly its Engineers, both mechanical and electrical. As early as 1921 the Colliery provided its own electricity, which benefited the local people who had their houses and streets installed with electricity at this early date. Also supplied with electricity were Morrison Terrace and Mainsforth Village. Many experiments were carried out both underground and on the surface with various types of machinery. In 1950 a steel underground roof supporting device, which became known as the Chock named after Mr Peter Kay the Colliery Manager, was developed by Mr Fred Kirkby, the foreman Welder. Although colliery pit head baths were reported as early as 1914 in the Lancashire coalfield, Mainsforth baths which were erected in the July of 1929 were amongst the earliest in Durham.

Mainsforth Colliery around 1910. North Terrace is to the left of the pit.

This photograph shows Tom Dixon aged $1^1/_2$ years standing with his father Tom in front of their 1938 Singer Saloon at Leasingthorne in 1942.

This lovely photograph of Tom Dixon aged 4 years old was taken at the Pictorial Studios, The Esplanade, Redcar on 15th September 1944. Standing beside him is his mother Terry Dixon, a well known business lady of Leasingthorne.

Another picture of Tom Dixon with his father Tom and grandfather Tom, better known to the Villagers as Old Tom, Young Tom and Young Tom's son. They are standing behind what looks like grandfather's prize cabbages, Leasingthorne 1941.

All lined up for the Saturday night hop, held in the local village hall, Leasingthorne *circa* 1950. Pictured here are: Unknown, Mrs Liddel, Edith Hopper, unknown and Mary Cartwright (local dressmaker).

Three beautiful children strolling along the footpaths between Oak and Ash Terraces, Leasingthorne. The photograph shows Valerie Donaldson between Harry Russell's young daughters.

Brotherly love, Cliff and Derrick Cartwright in the backyard of 14 Yew Terrace, Leasingthorne 1940. Note the rabbit hutch in the corner.

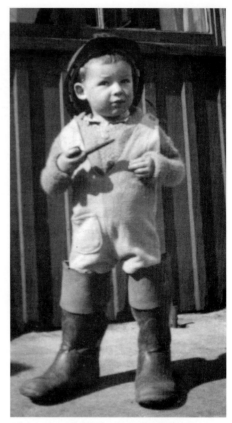

This wonderful photograph shows Barry Campbell aged two years, all dressed up in his father's wellington boots and pit helmet and firmly holding on to a clay pipe. Behind him is 14 Yew Terrace, Leasingthorne. These houses were finished at the front with wood cladding, clearly visible behind young Barry. As a consequence, these houses were known locally at the 'Wood Houses'. Photograph taken *circa* 1950s.

Bill Fairless would be about 2 years old when this photograph was taken of him sometime during the late 1920s early 1930s, dressed in his dad's jacket and cap. He looks as if he isn't too sure that he approves of it. The dog is obviously more interested in inspecting the pavement.

Very little information can be found about this photograph showing a group picture of members and officials outside Leasingthorne and District Workmen's Club and Institute at No 16 Eden Terrace, now a private residence.

Mr Ord of Dene Bridge Road, Chilton, seen here immaculate in his scout uniform, is believed to have been the first Scoutmaster of Chilton.

These images show Mr George Charlton, the well known village elder of Kirk Merrington. George as a small child all dressed up in his Sunday best, faces the photographer and from the expression on his face seems to be wondering how much longer to hold on. George

as a young boy stands outside Charlton's workshop, Kirk Merrington date 1918. Finally George poses proudly, wearing his first undertaker's outfit. He joined the family business on leaving school in 1924 and remained there until his retirement in 1992, this period of employment being broken only by his military service 1942-46. Sadly George passed away on 9th October 1998. I feel very proud that I had the chance to meet and spend some time with him. Like most people of his age he really had some stories to tell!

This lovely studio photograph of the Lidster family was taken at the Swiss Art Studio, Bishop Auckland in 1875. Mr Lidster was at the time the licensee of the Bay Horse Inn, Kirk Merrington, now a private residence.

Below: Another photograph of the Lidster family, this time at the rear of the Bay Horse Inn, Kirk Merrington *circa* 1879.

In this excellent and also unusual photograph, three young brothers, left to right: William, Thomas and John Lidster (bricklayers), stop to pose for the photographer. These young bricklayers were involved in the early stages of building Bede Place, Kirk Merrington in 1908. Note John, who is smoking a pipe.

Postcard showing William Lidster on the mounting steps outside the Fox and Hounds pub, Kirk Merrington with William Charlton standing alongside him *circa* 1908.

TRANSPORT

A steam wagon laden with timber owned by Thomas Golightly of Ferryhill with a group of workmen in the foreground. The wagon is standing in front of South View, opposite Manor Farm *circa* 1910. Note the cottages on the left with the lovely pantile roof.

Lettice (Letty) Thompson ready to go! The motor bike and sidecar belonged to her father Campbell Thompson and was parked outside No 4 Owen Street, Dean Bank, *circa* 1933. The iron footbridge at the end of the street leads across the Ferryhill 'Cut' towards Darlington Road.

Below: Outside 47 Newton Street, Dean Bank, Ferryhill in the late 1930s. Mr Isaac Raine and his wife Rosa were the owners of this Baby Austin 7 (Rosa is seen standing beside the car). The badge on the radiator grill shows they were members of the AA. UP on the number plate indicates a Durham registration.

Ferryhill – the young boy, William Cummings, aged 14-15 years out on his rounds with Co-operative Dairy horse and cart.

This vintage United bus is seen here fitted with an open upper deck. Operating a service on the Bishop Auckland, Ferryhill, Spennymoor route it is thought to be standing at the front of the Greyhound pub, Market Street, Ferryhill *circa* 1920s. The driver takes time to pose for this photograph as does the 'clippie' standing there in her dust coat holding on to her ticket machine. An absolute gem of a photograph; there is so much you can see in this picture.

A group of drivers and workmen in front of a Martindale's bus. This well known bus company ran a variety of services for many years around the Ferryhill area. Included in the picture are, left to right: Billy Curry, unknown, Ralph Carr, unknown and Billy Leng.

One of many trips which went from Ferryhill. This photograph shows a group of locals ready to board one of Preston's buses on an outing to Seaton Carew, from Thirlmere Road, Ferryhill in 1949. Left to right: Marjorie Williams, Beattie Brown, Doris McClean, Andrew Predki, Ellis Griffiths, Ida Chapman. (Doris & Andrew and Ellis & Ida later married.) Unfortunately the names of the two on the right are unknown.

The people of Ferryhill have been blessed with an excellent public transport system for many years, and it has often been said that you could catch a bus to anywhere from its market place. Two of the old companies of yesteryear that provided a great service were the ABC and the Favourite Services. Named after its proprietors, Messrs Arron, Binks and Coulson, the ABC ran from Feethams bus stop in Darlington via Ferryhill to Sunderland during the 1940/50s, when the village had three cinemas operating. The conductor would often shout from the bus steps 'Standing room only' or 'Sorry, no more room for passengers'. The Favourite Services ran an hourly service from Bishop Auckland via Ferryhill and Sedgefield to Stockton. Mr William Duffield of Bishop Middleham was the proprietor of this company. The business was run from Central Garage, a wood structure at the West end of Bishop Middleham Brewery, near the entrance leading to Well House.

Threshing at Mainsforth Colliery Farm.

G.W. Lazenby and Co Builders and Haulage Contractors, were the proud owners of this steam powered wagon, manufactured by Mann Patent Steam Carriage Wagon Co Ltd. This photograph was taken *circa* 1920s. Note the oil lamp and the water tank behind the cab. The photograph shows that it was probably taken in one of the local colliery pit yards as you can see part of the shaft headgear in the background. The letter J on the number plate indicates a County Durham registration.

Horse-drawn hearse photographed by Ian Yeoman of the *Sunday Times*. The row of single storey colliery houses was known as Stone Row, Leasingthorne. This row, together with Heap Row and Pit Row, was built in 1842 to form the original colliery village. Heap Row and Pit Row were demolished around 1944 but this row survived until 1976 before it too was demolished.

Another photograph of a horse-drawn hearse in front of Oak Terrace, Leasingthorne. These houses were of brick construction with distinctive wood cladding on the front and consequently often referred to as the 'Wood Houses'. Demolished *circa* 1964.

Sitting proudly on his Royal Enfield, Cliff Cartwright in his teens outside 14, Yew Terrace, Leasingthorne with his parents looking on, *circa* 1950s.

Looks like a busy day in one of the fields at Kirk Merrington, cutting corn with a Hornsby Self Binder pulled by two horses. As the saying goes 'many hands make light work', even the small children will have their tasks to fulfil.

Delivering milk in and around Ferryhill until 1950 was a far more personal job than today when deliveries are dropped at the doorstep. The milkman arrived every morning at each doorstep ready to fill the customer's jug or bowl with milk from his pint or gill measure, Pulled by horse, this Swaledale type milk float has been abandoned with its milk churns along the Ferryhill to Merrington road which has been blocked by drifting snow. One of the men may be a Mr Conway who was a coal miner. The ruins of Ferryhill Cornmill can be seen on the far left horizon. The mill operated until 1879-1880 when a man called Storey was the last miller there. He lived in a cottage near at hand to the mill which relied upon the wind for its source of power. The photograph is dated 30th January 1910. This was a Sunday which explains why the two men are not in their workclothes.

MINES AND RAILWAYS

A group of miners photographed outside the workshops at Dean and Chapter Colliery. Included in the group are: Morris Cox, Syd Turnbull and Albert Richardson.

Leasingthorne Colliery *circa* 1910 showing the ovens and tar works on the left with the coal screening plant and shaft headgear on the right. This was a two stage colliery, the original shafts being sunk in 1842-1843 to work the upper seams with new shafts sunk in 1901-1903 to work the lower seams. The second stage colliery was a larger unit having coke ovens, tar works and brickworks associated. The mine was originally owned by the Bolckow Vaughan Mining Co who merged with Dorman Long and Co in 1929. It remained in their possession until 1947 when it was taken over by the National Coal Board. At its peak some 1,000 men and boys were employed, producing around 300,000 tons of coal per annum. The colliery closed in 1965.

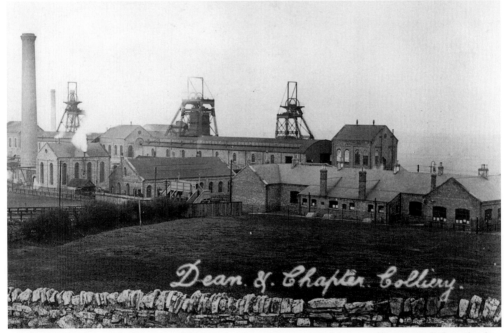

Views of Dean and Chapter Colliery, showing workshops, offices and the shaft headgear behind.

Ferryhill Dean and Chapter Colliery St John Ambulance Brigade team, winners of the NCB national competition in 1961 and the St John Ambulance Brigade competition in 1963. Here they are receiving a local award. Left to right: Area Coal Board Dr Pearson, Billy McAdam (Captain), Billy Wright, Lance Smith, George Kerry, Ralph Gibson and Jack Kellett.

Jack Curry of 8 Newton Street, Dean Bank, Ferryhill aged fourteen, ready to start his working life as a coal miner. This photograph was taken in front of the Brockwell No One Shaft at Dean and Chapter Colliery in 1919. There he worked alongside his father and two uncles who were coal hewers at the colliery and by the time Jack was 17 he was pony putting and coal hewing at 18. He then moved on to deputy work and progressed to a Master Shifter, Back Shift Overman and finally Fore Overman. After many years in the coal mine he had to retire in 1959 due to ill health. Sadly Jack died in 1963.

A colliery under official (deputy) adjusting his oil lamp while testing for gas on one of the Long Wall coal faces at Dean and Chapter Colliery in the 1950s. The length and height of the coal face seams that were operated by this method varied from between 1 foot to 4 foot in thickness and anywhere from 100-200 yards long. Approximately 24 inches in height, this coal seam roof of stone is supplied by steel straps which show three methods of roof support: on the left, the steel chock which was released by a steel wedge, centre the timber prop and right the Dowty hydraulic prop operated by oil and released by a square socket key.

View taken at the coal face, Dean and Chapter Colliery during the 1950-1960s. The Mothergate or Roadhead is at the centre of operations in extracting coal by the Long Wall Method, by virtue of the fact that it is the main intake for the rail track, the main gate conveyor and it provides the fresh air. This classic photograph shows a 12 foot by 8 foot Mothergate complete with steel arch girders supporting the road head roof. (Note the stilts or wood props at the foot of each of the girders. As the roof subsides due to pressure from above these close).

Dean and Chapter Colliery Band *circa* 1950. This photograph was taken outside Dean Bank School, Ferryhill. Among those in the picture are: Mr Tommy Fodden, Mr Mattie Fodden, Teddy Shields and his son George, Harry Wilkinson, Mr T. Selby, Mr Brown, Mr E. Elms, Mr J. Jones, Mr H. McCavanagh, J. Vickerstaff, Mr McCadam, Mr Scott and Mattie Fodden's young son, Malcolm, holding the bugle.

Mr Tom Fodden centre with his sons – Tom on his right and Mattie on his left, standing outside 13 Paxton Street, Dean Bank, Ferryhill *circa* 1945. All were members of the Dean and Chapter Colliery Band, The photographer was S. Blaylock, 73 High Street, Spennymoor.

Dean and Chapter Colliery Ambulance Team, 1930. Back row: Billy Butterfield, Billy Alderson, Lance Smith, Jack Priestnell, George Kerry. Front row: Mr Fogan – Colliery Manager from Stirling, Scotland, Don Kerry (Captain) and Mr Mather.

Dean and Chapter Ambulance Men in the 1940s proudly showing the Dorman Long, Corona Graham and other shields in the pit yard. The workshop buildings and shaft headgear are behind. Back row: Lance Smith, Billy Wright and George Kerry. Front row: Billy McAdam, Donald Kerry and Billy Alderson.

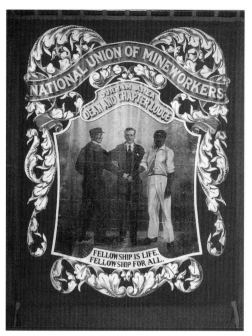

Dean and Chapter Colliery Miners'
Lodge Banner which now hangs in
the Town Hall, Ferryhill Village.

Mainsforth Colliery Miners' Lodge
Banner which also hangs in the Town
Hall, Ferryhill Village.

Gloria Bruce and Margaret Hymers standing in front of the NUM Lodge Banner
of Dean and Chapter Colliery, shortly after it had been paraded into Durham
City and onto the Racecourse on Durham Miners' Gala Day in 1960.

Retired Dean and Chapter Colliery mineworkers receiving food parcels from the Perth (Australia) Red Cross Society in 1942–43. In the background are the winding gears above the three shafts of the colliery.

Picture showing Mr Robert Spooner holding one of Dean and Chapter's pit ponies 'Barny' after returning from the Royal Horse Show at Cambridge in 1951 with the title 'Champion Pit Pony'. Alongside him is Mr Hugill the head horse keeper with Mr Dick Cockfield – all are looking very pleased with their awards.

Officials and a policeman at the Dean and Chapter Colliery, Ferryhill, distributing coal rations to strikers during the 1921 Strike.

Mainsforth Colliery *circa* 1920. The shafts were sunk in 1876–77 to the Harvey Seam by the Carlton Iron Company, following a failed earlier attempt abandoned after contacting major water feeders. The colliery closed about four years after opening and remained so until 1904, when it was re-opened and the shafts deepened to the Brockwell Seam. Around 1923 the mine was taken over by Dorman Long and Co who retained possession until 1947 when the industry was Nationalised. At its peak, some 2,300 men and boys were employed, producing around 740,000 tons of coal per annum. The colliery officially closed in December 1968 although a small amount of coal was produced in 1969 during salvage operations.

Dene Bridge/Chilton Colliery. The shafts were sunk by Messrs Pease and Partners in 1872-73 to the Main Coal Seam and deepened in two later stages, 1879 to the Harvey Seam and 1882 to the Brockwell Seam. It was taken over by Dorman Long and Co around 1934 in whose possession it remained until Nationalisation in 1947. At its peak, some 1,500 men and boys were employed producing around 450,000 tons of coal per annum. The colliery closed in 1965

This photograph of Dean and Chapter Colliery, *circa* 1910 gives some indication of the size of the mine with two of its three shafts showing and a large surface layout. The photograph also shows the old Great North Road winding past the brewery before climbing the steep hill into Ferryhill Village. The colliery was sunk in 1902-04 and was the largest and most modern in the area. At its peak some 2,600 men and boys were employed, producing around 750,000 tons of coal per annum. It was originally owned by the Bolckow Vaughan Mining Company who in 1929 merged with Dorman Long and Company, in whose possession it remained until 1947, when it was taken over by the National Coal Board. The colliery closed in 1966.

Windlestone Colliery *circa* 1906.
Two views showing the fine timber
headgear to the mainshaft along
with the winding house. They also
shows the impressive chimney
used for raising steam, the driving
face for the colliery winding
engines and most other colliery
machinery. Sunk in 1876-77 for
Messrs Pease and Partners, the
main shaft was sunk to the
Ganister Seam some 323 feet below
the Brockwell and bored a further
195 feet, looking for additional
workable coal seams, without
success. In the late 1880s.
following a collapse in coal prices,
the mine was 'laid idle' and
remained so until around 1895.
During this period of closure
Windlestone Village became almost
deserted. After the re-opening of
the mines, the village again
prospered until 1931, when
following another collapse in coal
prices, the colliery was again 'laid
idle'; this time it never re-opened.

The 'Leeholme' Loco No 120 0-4-0 Works No 2916 built by Hawthorn Leslie in 1912 and scrapped in 1923, after a very short working life for the colliery. This may suggest that it was involved in some kind of accident. It was passed on to Dorman Long on 1st November 1929.

Loco No 102 Saddle Tank built by Hawthorne Leslie in 1900, Works No 2449. Worked for Balckow Vaughan and Co until 1st November 1929 and then Dorman Long until it was scrapped in 1937. Seen here with a group of workers at Leasingthorne Colliery.

This Leasingthorne Colliery Loco No 110, Works No 2654 Saddle Tank was built by Hawthorne Leslie in 1906. It worked for Balckow Vaughan and Co up to 1st November 1929 when it was transferred to Chilton Colliery, remaining there until 1st November 1947.

Leasingthorne Colliery Prize Band. They were the winners of the first wireless contest in 1926 and the tune they played was 'Oberon'. Included in the picture are: Tommy Smith, Manny Smith, Billy Hutchinson, Benny Smith, Ernie Ellison, Phil Wigley, Percy Smith, Jimmy Scofield, Albert Wigley, Alfie Coates, Ned Wigley, Danny Teasdale, John Temperley, Emanuel Smith, Joe Dayton, Alfred McLean and his son Archie.

Thomas Raine 21st Lancer in 1918, stands proud for the photographer during his wartime years.

The same Thomas Raine from the previous photograph some 19 years later standing on the right with Eddie Milner alongside him and seated, left to right: Mr Bushby and Jack Gallacher, all miners from Leasingthorne Colliery during their stay at Conishead Priory, a convalescent home for injured and sick miners.

Below: Conishead Priory – depicted on Mainsforth Colliery Lodge Banner – which overlooks Morecambe Bay. Situated deep in the Lake District, the Priory lies a few miles to the South of Ulverston. Durham Miners' Association bought the Priory in August 1930 and turned it into a convalescent home for injured and sick miners. It was about this time that the 7.5 hours Coal Mines Act was passed whereby a man working underground was due to work a 7.5 hour shift. Extremely proud of their National Union of Mineworkers' Lodge Banner, each July Mainsforth and Bishop Middleham men with their wives and families gathered around the banner for entry into Durham City on the day of the Miners' Gala, which was considered to be one of the greatest shows on earth. There are many stories and tales of hardship and struggle that the miners endured in the early days before the Durham Miners' Association was formed 1869–70, to be followed later by the National Union of Mineworkers in 1945.

A general view of Ferryhill railway station goods yards with Mainsforth Colliery behind. In 1834, the Clarence Railway was the first rail company to use the Ferryhill Gap for its mineral line from Port Clarence to Coxhoe. In 1844 the Newcastle and Darlington Junction Railway ran another line alongside, using the same natural gap in the hills. Whilst use was made of the gap, some 100,000 cubic yards of rock were removed to obtain the required width and gradient. The section of line between Ferryhill and Relly Mill (South of Durham) was opened to passengers in 1872. This was followed in June 1887 by the opening of the spacious island station at Ferryhill, at a cost of £13,612, the outer faces being used by through trains, with bay platforms left in at each end for local trains. The station closed in 1967 and was demolished in 1969.

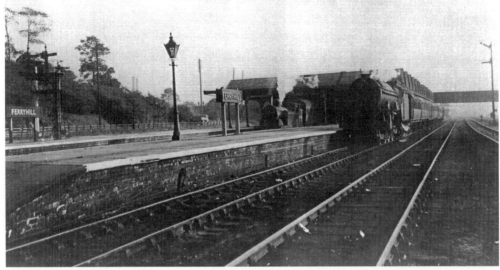

'The Age of Steam' standing at the platform at Ferryhill railway station.

These two photographs show the slender iron pillars supporting the well designed iron and glass roofing over the platforms.

Billy Dunn, aged 8 years with his dogs, Lassie and Wolf sitting alongside East Howle railway crossing and signal box in 1964. Not long after this photograph was taken the railway crossing and signal box were demolished. Pine Road can be seen in the distance top right.

We end this section on mining with this typical group of pitmen standing on the gantry, ready to go down the mine. Photographed at Leasingthorne Colliery *circa* 1929. Five of the men are holding battery operated lamps while Larry Gordon, the man on the far right, is holding an oil filled lamp which was used for testing for gas underground. Left to right: John Kerry, John Catterson, Jack Catterson, Mr Walton, unknown and Larry Gordon.

SCHOOLDAYS

A happy group of children from Dean Bank School outside the Wheatsheaf Hotel, Ferryhill prior to departing for a day out at the seaside *circa* 1928.

Dean Bank Council School, Ferryhill. Built in 1907, the school had separate boys and girls departments. Remarkably little in this picture has changed.

Dean Bank Infants School 1950s. Back row: Ann Gough, Pat Forrest, Vera Williams and Avril Blenkinsop. Middle row: Ann Barber, Ann Weaver, Denise Owen, Janice Jowett, Betty Gillham, Christine Thompson, Ann Wayman, Marie Brewis and Rosemary Tills. Front row: Brenda Joyce, Elizabeth Norton, Elizabeth Knowles, Dorothy Ashett, Sonia Cheesebrough, Rosalind Cheesebrough, Mrs Elgey (teacher), Dulcie Dawson, unknown, Pamela Wren, Pauline Griffith, Enid Whittaker and Lynn Crawford.

Dean Bank Junior School 1949. Among those in the picture are, back row: Doreen Thompson, Jacqueline Burke, Maureen Caffery, Marjory Henderson, Margaret Stevenson, Eileen Farnaby, Betty Forest. Second row: Audrey Littely, Jean McKinen, Sylvia Meek, Mabel Todd, Iris Stairmond, Ann Stevenson, Valerie Rimmer, Mary Horner, Brenda Hodgson. Third row: Betty Nolan, Betty Horner, Jean Lee, Ann Carr, Elizabeth Copper, unknown, Ann Leonard, Judith Ward, unknown, Eileen Jones, Amelia Heal. Front row: Dorothy Hill, Gwen Jones, Thelma Beavis, Audrey Clear, Merle Dunn, Mrs Dennison (Music Teacher), Jean Morphet, Ann Cheesmond, unknown, Brenda Peart and Renie Houston.

Dean Bank Boys School 1950 Senior 3. Back row: J. Charlton, F. Gray, P. Collins, R. Shenton, E. Beavis, J. Jones, P. Neasham, J. Cook, D. Healy, B. Toas. Middle row: K. Wood, J. Young, C. Dixon, C. Bowron, D. Gibson, R. Cousins, J. Gleghorn, F. Batey, S. Kears, W. Atkinson. Front row: E. Higgins, J. Tregoning, D. Viningham, W. Anderson, B. Wrightson, J. Durkin (Teacher), R. Peg, K. Griffin, W. McCrickard, J. Ivenson, A. Jermy.

Dean Bank Junior School – Class 4A, *circa* 1959. Back row: Jacqueline Daniels, Brenda Steele, Rita Robson, Pam Devonport, Anna Beale, Barbara Hird, Flora Douglas, Sheila Howe, Vivien Howard, unknown, Audrey Beeton, Pat Rothery, Marion Leng, Lynne Rayner. Middle row: Lesley Rutherford, Diane Hartley, Maureen Hutchinson, Jean Guthrie, Jean Robinson, Bernice Murphy, Jeanete Walker, Susan Lancaster, Jean Hudson, Margaret Halton, Anne Pride, Jean Kennedy, Jean Simpson. Front row: Sylvia Payne, Christine Farnaby, Audrey James, Julia Douglas, Karen Wrightson, Jean Welsh, Miss Sotheran (Teacher), Margaret Donals, Winifred Leonard, Linda Swinbank, Margaret Sherriff, Pauline Madden, Jacqueline Neasham.

Opposite page:

Music lesson outside Dean Bank Infants School 1945. One of my favourite photographs absolutely bursting with happiness. You can see the delight on every child's face. In the back row are: Albert Goundry, Eric Dent, Laurence Hall, Colin Henderson, Gordon Harris, Kenny Williams, Jimmy Brown, Victor Lamb, Brian Sherlock, Robert Nicholson, Barbara Burdess, Raymond Batey, Paul Turnbull, Ken Hamilton, John King, Iris Burdess, Ann Carr, Billy Crawford, Iris Redfearn, Barbara Proud, Sheila Bell. Front row: Ann Rothwell, Betty Nolan, Joyce Stebbins, Anita Curry, Enid Forster, Barbara Curry, Tom Brackwell, Josephine Heath, Marry Topping, Jean Morphet, Alan Gamsby, Mary Oyston, Alice Graham, Reggie Oliver, unknown, Maurice Jones.

DEAN BANK INFANTS 1945.

This school production of 'The Snow Queen' took place at Dean Bank School, Ferryhill in 1959. Seen here are youngsters of Dean Bank School. Amongst those taking part are: Marjorie Eddy, Anne Predki, Lynn Myers, Brenda Flannagan, Janet Hudson, Ian Etherington and Lesley Garnett.

Cleves Cross School, Ferryhill – Halloween Concert. Included are: Samantha McKenna, Andrew Thompson, Neil Kisby, Lee Harwood, Vannesa Etherington, Nigel Holmes, Lee Nevison, Julie Cason, Andrew Cockburn, Michael Boran, Andrea Campbell, John Paul Thompson, Nicola Wright, Christine Jones, Stephanie Flockett, Lee Smith, Jason Hartnell, Regan Harle, Joanna Armstrong, Paul Cason and Angela Lowry.

Cleves Cross School, Ferryhill Christmas Pantomine in 1978. Some of those included are: Nicola Eggleston, Tina Cunningham, Penny Rothwell, Allison Turner, Suzanne Stark, Ann Johnsonton, Julie Taylor, Linda Pearson, Kay Stannard, Julie Bell, Andrea Roddam, Nicola Greenland and Jill Warrior.

Cleves Cross School in December 1978. A fine selection of Egyptian dancers at the school performance of Alladin.
Seen here are: Tina Hockworth, Alison Bell, Suzanne Greenland, Gillian Tate, Angela Lamb, Julian Quinn, Lisa Laverick and Tracy Fenwick.

Ferryhill Station School celebrate 'The Relief of Mafeking' in 1900.

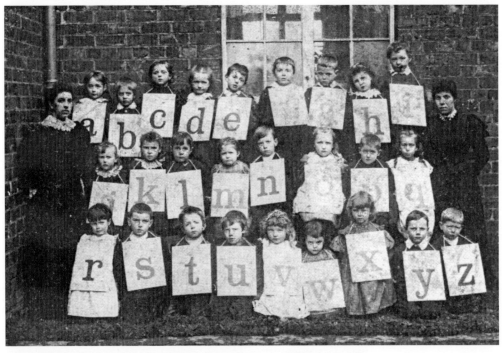

Ferryhill Station School Infants classes, *circa* 1900.

Staff from East Howle School *circa* 1920. Back row: Doris Marshall, Nellie Miller, unknown, unknown, unknown. Front row: unknown, Dan Wallace, Miss Maxi, John George Adamson (Headmaster), Agnes Adamson (Headmistress).

Nativity scene performed by the children of East Howle School, Ferryhill early 1950s and only one person identified – Gloria Bruce, the small child sitting down to the right of baby Jesus.

A class photograph of East Howle Council Mixed School, Group V taken in 1920. The school closed in the late 1960s.

Little is known about the children seen here other than that they call themselves the Chilton Minstrels and were photographed outside the school building in the school yard in 1914.

Chilton Buildings Council School from a card postmarked 1912. This school is a familiar landmark to many people who drive through on the Old A1 (now the A167). The school was officially opened on 1st September 1909 by J.L. Shirlaw esq JP. The boys and girls departments were independent of each other, even having separate playgrounds.

The official opening of Kirk Merrington Primary School *circa* 1928. Among those in the picture are: Thomas Conlon (Scoutmaster), Mr Dougall (headmaster), W. Raine (Chapel preacher), Jack Askew (village shop owner), Mrs Sharp (newsagent), Mr Scurr (farmer), Billy Hall (farmer), Mrs Raine, Mrs Ward, Mr Summerson, Mrs Brown and Mr Askew.

Leasingthorne School Group *circa* 1953. The teachers are Miss Chegwin and Mr Smith and known pupils include: Brian Williams, Alan Russell, John Benson, Denis Jordan, Jean Benson, Pauline Preston, Carol Rennolds, Pauline Slee, Faith Mills, William Oliver, Norman Williams, Gordon Elliott, Marion Errington, Jean Errington, Derick Young, Keith Benson, Ruth Weatherell, Keith Pinder, Kenneth Wright, Keith Calvert, Lilian Weatherell, Geraldine Williams, Jeffery Errington, Stuart Morton, Valerie Williams, Sylvia Benson, David Rennolds, Marion Oliver, Eric Maughan, Arthur Murrey, Hazel White, Yvonne Smith, Tom Slee, Ann Stobbs, Joyce Stobbs and Jacqueline Campbell.

SECTION SIX

SPORT

Ferryhill Athletic Football Team, 1949. Standing: L. Malone, unknown, R. Bell, Jess Potts, unknown, F. Ridley. Kneeling: Joe Carr, Jimmy McCormack, Albert Flocket, unknown, Billy Leng. Photograph taken on Home Ground, Darlington Road. Their strip was black and amber.

Dean Bank Cricket Team photographed outside the Club Pavilion in the 1950s.
Front row: Ralph Wilson, unknown, Syd Turnbull, unknown, Ernie Redfearn.
Back row: Unknown, unknown, Arthur Strachan, Billy Surtees, Tommy
Swainston, unknown, unknown.

A quiet spoken, unassuming man, Bill Gibbons is a gentleman in every sense of the word. A family man with two sons, Brian and Neil, he married Jean Carr who worked for many years in the village post office at Ferryhill. Other than his family, the two great passions in his life are football and a love of the countryside. Now in his eighties, Bill is one of Ferryhill Athletics grand old men, who can look back with nostalgia to those early days both before the Second World War and afterwards into the 1950s when he played inside left position for the team and with fellow team mates thrilled the Darlington Road crowd whose roar could be heard half way down the Broom Road bank. The photograph shows Bill during his army days in the Second World War.

Ferryhill won the Northern League Challenge Cup during the 1947-1948 season beating the mighty 'Bishops', Bishop Auckland 2-1 in the final. Bill Gibbons scored one of the winning goals which saw him and fellow team mates take the Winners medals. He counts his winner's medal as one of his proud possessions marking the occasion of that thrilling day more than half a century ago.

Dean Bank Boys, 1950– 51. Winning Team for Spennymoor District School Shield and Cup for Dean Bank Aged Miners'. Back row: Mr Hetherington, C. Laidler, R. Cooper, D. Vaulks, E. Bevis, R. Cutmore, A. Hopper, D. Golightly, Mr Gregson. Front row: R. Rothwell, R. Blair, D. Gibson, A. Morland, A. Todd.

Bob Welsh aged 16 years old at the Mainsforth Cricket ground, Ferryhill Station *circa* 1933. Bob was brought up in the family home on Mainsforth Road, quite near to the present sports complex. At the Ferryhill Station School, he was a keen player for both the cricket and the football teams. From the age of 9 to the present day (he's now 85) he has been keenly connected with the Mainsforth Cricket Club system. He also played football for Spennymoor United Club. After retiring from playing, he acquired his umpire's certificate and then trained at New College, Durham as a cricket coach. Now, in 2001, he is president of his favourite club.

He began his working life as an apprentice colliery mechanic, becoming a mobile mechanic of the mines, and retired as the collieries began to close in Northumberland and Durham.

For many years he has been a member of Ferryhill Rowlandson Lodge of Freemasons and has now been made an honorary member. During his 60 years of marriage he has been a Methodist Church member, and with his wife Freda in the late 1940s ran a very successful youth club in the Westcott Chapel. He was one of the familiar members of the Broom Aged People's Welfare, the Ferryhill TOC H, Ferryhill Age Concern and Ferryhill Fellowships of Churches. Bob was also a sport correspondent for the 'Evening Despatch' and for the 'Pink'.

For over 40 years, since the birth of their handicapped only child, the couple have done endless voluntary work to try to enhance the lives of all disabled children. At present, Bob is a member of the Ferryhill Advisory Group of the Health Alliance.

Dean Bank Juniors, 1952-53. Committee Members, left to right: A. Straughan, Mr Spedding (Chemist), W. Johnson, J. Charlton, W. Straughan, B. Clear, A. Bellwood, M. McCourt, G. Foster, Dennis Watson. Middle row: D. Hunter, Lonsdale, A. Morland, M. Green, P. Dickinson. Front row: J. Gleghorn, A. Gardener, G. Austin, T. Slater, R. Blair, J. Vickerstaff. G. Austin is holding the Bishop Auckland Challenge Cup.

Dean Bank Ferryhill Juniors, 1954-55. Back row: Mr Hetherington, J. Gates, D. Franklin, L. Walker, B. Metcalfe, K. Brown, R. Woods, D. Varty and Mr Ford. Front row: T. Rounsley, I. Gordon, W. Gates, B. Shaw and J. Heaviside.

St Luke's Church Ferryhill, Tennis Club *circa* 1920 with Mr Joe McManners. A lay preacher at St Luke's, Mr McManners eventually joined the priesthood, becoming vicar at West Pelton before succeeding Canon Lomax as Vicar of St Luke's when the Canon retired in 1940.

A group of teenagers from St Luke's Tennis Club, Ferryhill, *circa* 1930s seen here with Canon Lomax and his wife outside the vicarage. Mr Billy Alderson of Ferryhill took the photograph.

Cleves Cross School football team photographed in 1981 at the school with Mr John Hepplewhite, the headmaster. Back row: Michael Bowron, Stephen Kell, Reagan Harle, Andrew Thompson, Gareth Fodden and Lee Rankin. Middle row: Andrew Malcolm, John Thompson, David Cockburn, Dean McKenna and Ian Willets. Front row: Jason Hartnell and Alister Gardiner.

A football match in progress on the playing fields below East Howle School, probably taken in the early 1900s. The school closed in the mid 1960s.

East Howle Football Team, 1946. Back row: Stan Ball, Eric Marshall, Alec Mason, Bill Fairless, Eric Christlow. Front row: Ernest Ward, Dennis Booth, Warwick Wallace, Jim Ramsey, Alan Pratt. Mile Halpen (centre front) proudly holding the ball.

Mainsforth Cricket Club late 1940s/early 1950s seen here with the Matthew Oswald Cup. Back row: W. Little, R. Cole, J. Chesterton, W. Foster, M. Noakes, H. Taylor, R. Welsh, E. Bell (secretary), J. Honeyball. Front row: E. Hall, D. Patchett, L. Patterson, T. Honeyball, G. Moore, A Greenwood.

Mainsforth Colliery Cricket Team, 1951. Those standing include: Eddie Bell, Arthur Wood, Derek Nobbs, Billy Blenkinsop, David Blair, Kit Willey, John Gibson. Seated: John Wayman, John Wheaton, Jake Taylor, Ron Allison, unknown.

Mainsforth Dean and Chapter cricketers at the Old Cricket Ground at 'Dicky Pit' Dean and Chapter Colliery, September 1938. The Mid Durham Senior League played a team from the staff of the Northern Echo. Left to right: T. Welford, J. Rivers, R. Rothwell, F. Welsh, J. Cooper (captain), R. Gibson, S. Turnbull, S. Leighton, R. Welsh, W. Walton, W. Surtees, J. Dobson (umpire).

Mainsforth Football Team, *circa* 1943. Back row: T. Ashett, T. Flatman, T. Mudd, B. Nelson, R. Bell. Middle row: R. Richardson, A. Gobin, J. Blair, T. Smailes, unknown, T.E. Bell. Front row: W. Mathews, A. Wallace, A. Mathews, W. Davison, R. Anderson, J. Price.

A game of bowls at Dean Bank Recreation Ground, Ferryhill, *circa* 1950. The only person to be identified in this picture is Mr Tom Winter, the gentleman in the foreground wearing a suit and trilby hat.

EVENTS AND OCCASIONS

Youngsters here seem to be enjoying celebrating VE Day in Church Lane, Ferryhill Village, 1945. The lady in the long black coat is Charlotte Goundrey. Behind her is her daughter Jennie. The children sitting on the donkey holding on tight are: John Simpson, Peter Hall with his mother standing behind, Chris Shaw, Tommy McCartin. Mr Bailes of Manor Farm kindly loaned them the donkey for the day and the young girl standing at the rear end of the donkey is Irene Holt.

All in fancy dress, possibly celebrating VE Day in Thirlmere Road, Ferryhill in 1945. Shown in this photograph: Doris McLean, Doreen Etherington, Ella Trotter, Malcolm Porter, Eric Johns, Maurice Trotter, Mary Garnett, Nancy McLean and Nancy Heaviside. Note the two men at the back are in uniform, probably home on leave and joining in the celebrations. This is another photograph taken by keen photographer Harrison McLean.

Ferryhill Village, 1945. A street party taken in front of Hurford Terrace, now known as Church Lane, celebrating VE Day. Among those in the picture are: Jennie McCartin, Tommy McCartin, Irene Holt, Ena Cornforth, Jennie Goundrey, Maggie Robinson and her twins Maisie and Dorothy, Maggie Liddle, Emily Sterling and Mrs Carson and her daughter Linda. Everyone contributed towards making the party a successful event to the extent of Mr Simpson (one of the organisers) walking to Spennymoor some 2.5 miles away to buy ice cream from Alonzi's to bring back for the children.

A photograph of Members of the 27th Platoon E Company, 15th Battalion Durhams Local Home Guard outside the Town Hall, Ferryhill probably taken around 1944.

Dean and Chapter St John Ambulance Cadets in the early 1940s. Among those in the picture are, back row: J. Oxley, A. Little, R. Campion, unknown, S. Taylor, B. Higgins, unknown, R. Scott. Middle row: unknown, M. McAdams, H. Johnson, T. Selby, unknown, R. Robinson, A. Summers, H. Leonard, I. Hutchinson, H. Hugill. Front row: J. Hope, Ron Heath, unknown, J. Norton, unknown, T. Salmon, Reg Heath.

Ferryhill Auxiliary Fire Service, winners of the Sedgefield Area Cup Competition, 7th August 1941. Photograph taken outside Darlington Road Fire Station. Among those in the picture are: Mr Latheron, Eddie Carfort, Mr Fowler, Joe Cross, Mr Etherington, Albert Cooper, Mr Williams, Mr Graham, Mr Brewis, Mr Bird, Billy Moore, Dick Etherington, Mr Ramage. Kneeling, on the right is Billy Moore's younger brother and, on the left, Mr Fowler's younger brother.

Recreation Ground, Dean Bank, Ferryhill *circa* 1936 showing the Band Stand and in the background the Dean and Chapter Colliery Miners' Houses.

Gala day at Dean Bank Recreation Ground. The ladies' hats and dresses suggest the early 1900s.

The Touring Club of the Post Boy, Ferryhill seen here in the late 1930s, prior to departing on a weekend away. Among those in the picture are: Joe Golightly, Mr Ward, Mr Hodgeson, Teddy Humphrey, Mr Moore, Joe Pedington and Mr Chaytors.

Celebrating VE Day in Stephenson Street, Dean Bank, Ferryhill in 1945.
Included in this group are, front row: Unknown, Syd Turnbull, Harold
Waterworth. Middle row: Mrs Richards, unknown, unknown, unknown, Ena
Waterworth, unknown. Back row: Unknown, unknown, Mr Croft, Mrs Croft,
Mr Ellis, unknown.

This picture shows some of the members of the Dean Bank Women's Institute
circa 1953. Included in the group are: Katy Croft, Mrs Simpson, Mrs Crosbie,
Mrs Perry, Mrs Lamb, Adie Oswald, Mrs Iveson, Ethel Angus, Elizabeth Lowes
and Nora Smith.

Stephenson Street, Dean Bank, Ferryhill. This may be a group photograph to commemorate Queen Elizabeth II Coronation, 2nd June 1953. The ladies have just been presented with what looks like Ringtons tea caddies. Among those in the picture are: Mrs Hodgson, Mrs Gedling, Mrs Fodden, Mrs Kennedy.

Ferryhill Mother's Club in 1963. A presentation to Nurse Lowes (2nd from the right) after 25 years service at the Ferryhill Surgery. Amongst those in the photograph are: Doris Predki, Valeria Tweedy, Jean Collins, Brenda Caygill, Nora Varty, Joan Stothard and Rene Bennett.

Bridge End, Ferryhill Station clearly showing the monument to Mr Lamb who represented Ferryhill Station on the Sedgefield Rural District Council from 1895 to 1910, during the last three years of which he acted as Chairman of that body. Born in 1855, died 1910. The monument was erected by public subscription.

A closer view of the Monument to John Lamb at Ferryhill Station.

Inside Mainsforth Colliery Welfare Institute, Ferryhill Station in the 1950s. Twenty of the Mainsforth Women's Institute members are captured on camera. Included are: Lydia Reay, Cissy Williams, Rita Pearce, Mary Buck, Mrs Kelly, Jennie Smith and Lydia Rothwell, Mrs Smith, Edna Williams, Nancy Stonely, Alice Bell, Sadie Gill, Lily Hepple and Rhoda Reilly, Olive Chaplin, Bella Campbell, Mrs A. Spey and daughter Margaret and Mary Reay.

A scene from 'The Pied Piper of Hamlin', May 1955 at the Children's Theatre inside Mainsforth Miners' Welfare Hall, Ferryhill Station showing John Wright as the Pied Piper and Grant Wilkinson as the lame boy.

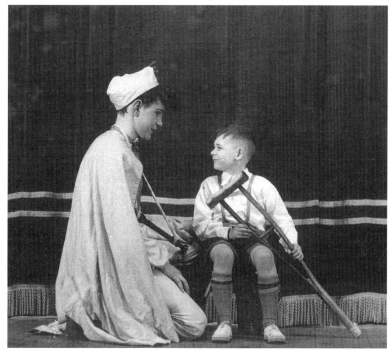

Members of the Mainsforth Colliery Silver Band pictured here at the junction of Gypsy Lane and Chilton Lane, Ferryhill Station on Durham Miners' Gala Day 21st July 1953.

The DMA Lodge Banner of Dean and Chapter Colliery with supporters outside the Black Bull Hotel probably preparing to march with their banner to parade in Durham City on Gala Day. The tall boy in the foreground (right) is holding a wooden crake which when swung vigorously would produce a very loud unpleasant noise.

CHURCHES AND CHAPELS

This lovely group of children pose proudly for the photographer inside the Broom Sunday School sometime in the 1940s. Standing at the back are Mr Avery, Mr Forster and Bessie Milner. Among the children seen here are: Fred Wilkinson, Shirley Brewster, Alan Smith, Jean Brittain, Brian Slater, Norman Flatman, Eric Brown, Margaret Staley, Pamela Devonport, Christine Heathcote, Malcolm Foddon, Bobby Spooner, Graham Gill, Derek Parnaby, Neil Garget, John Milner, Ian Brown, Keith Marley, Christine Stephenson, Diane Hartley, Jean Peverley, Maureen Peverley, Marilyn Ewin, Brian Avery, Catherine Tate, Jean Midgely, Desmond Ewen, Elizabeth Slater, Jennifer Welford, Margaret College, Kenneth Wilson, Jeffrey Gregg, Rita Robson, Edwin Robson, Margaret Tate, Margaret Sherriff, Michael Stevenson and Grant Wilkinson. I hope that many of the children shown in this photograph will be able to recognise themselves.

Children's Foundation Ceremony at the Zion Primitive Methodist Church, Dean Bank, Ferryhill, 13th April 1907. A marvellous display of hats among the ladies and small girls and everyone in their best attire. In the background can be seen the back of one of the new rows of colliery houses built by the owners of the recently sunk Dean and Chapter colliery to house the influx of miners and their families.

Members of the Zion Women's Own, inside the Zion Chapel, Dean Bank, Ferryhill *circa* 1967. Included in the group are: Mrs Jones, Doris Wright, Mrs Fox, Frances Brewis, Mrs Newton, Mrs Gleghorn, Mrs Mawson, Mrs Wade, Mrs Wilson, Sally Davis, Mrs Beverley, Mrs Longstaff, Lily McLean, Mrs Armstrong, Isa Tarn, Lizzie Romley and Edna Hunter.

St Luke's Parish Church, Ferryhill from the South East side. The church which was consecrated by the Bishop of Durham on 20th September 1853, replaced the former St Luke's which stood to the East end of the Market square. Note the bell tower in which there were two bells.

Incumbents:

Rev David Bruce, 1849-64
Rev H. Frederick Long, 1864-87
Rev Arthur J. Williams, 1887-95
Canon Thomas L. Lomax, 1895-1940
Canon Joseph McManners, 1940-52
Rev Ernest Johnson, 1952-62
Rev R. Wears, 1962-81
Rev Peter Baldwin, 1982-86
Rev Keith Lumsden, 1987–present

Canon Thomas Leech Lomax.

All Saints RC Church, Ferryhill. The new parish of All Saints was formed 1st November 1925 and the church opened 21st June 1927 due in no small way to the dedication of the first parish priest, Father J.L. Power.

Incumbents:

Fr Joseph Leo Power, 1st November 1925 until death on 23rd December 1943
Fr William Malone, 1944-50
Fr (later Canon) Lewis Landreth, 1950-53
Fr Edward Urquhart, 1953-73
Fr Bernard P Smith, 1973-80
Fr Patrick McGuigan, 1980-86
Fr Cornelius Horan, 1986-94
Fr Ronald Richmond, 1994-99
Fr Brian Murphy, 1999-present

Fr Joseph Leo Power.

Members of All Saints CWL, Ferryhill pictured here with Father Urqhart in the old church hall. The occasion is unknown. Included are: Father Urqhart, Mrs Sarah Toones, Mrs Dunlavey, Mrs A. Dunlavey, Mrs M. Leadbitter, Mrs Flynn, Mrs M. Barber, Mrs N. Abbot, Mrs M. McCartin, Mrs B. Kelly, Mrs Smallman, Mrs V. Espin, Mrs W. Quinn, Mrs N. Robinson, Mrs K. Conroy, Mrs J. McCartin, Mrs M. Moan and Mrs W. Stott.

The wedding of Miss Margaret Moan and Mr Alec Freak standing in the grounds of all Saints RC Church, Dean Road, Ferryhill. The priest is Father (later Canon) Lewis Landreth who was Parish Priest from 1950–1953.

Cannon Lomax's curates ready to entertain their audience with joyful song and probably some merriment as well. Among those in the group are: Rev Tuesday, Rev David Burney, Rev R. Burt and Rev Jack Shannon.

A group of All Saints RC youngsters in a dance and drama production. Back row: Margaret Price, Vera Corrigan, Monica Jefferson, Nora Garrigan. Front row: Jimmy Callan, George Whitfield, Gerrard Garrigan, Jimmy Wellan. The date and location unknown and the author would welcome further information.

Mr Sydney Brown, of Brompton Terrace, Dean Bank, Ferryhill and members of the Dean and Chapter Colliery Welfare Cricket Club and his bride, Miss Gladys Watts, of 4 Wolseley Street, Ferryhill Station, pass under an archway of cricket bats after their wedding at Ferryhill Village Methodist Church, *circa* 1950s. Others include: Syd Turnbull, George Allinson and Billy Surtees.

A programme for the production of a 'A Prince for Cinderella'. A Church group production of Cinderella involving youngsters at a concert performance held in the Broom Chapel in the 1960s. Back row: Fred Wilkinson, June Wilson, Ann Chapman. Front row: Ann Stoddard and Carol Stoddard.

A choir practice inside the Methodist Church Hall, Ferryhill Station late 1930s showing Mr James Myers conductor and pianists Olive Ford and Mr Arthur Lewis. Included in the choir: Mary Harley, Edna Lewis, Freda Stirk, Eva Ball, Jean White, Nancy Stephenson, Mrs Myers, Arthur Elliott, Billy Veitch, Edith Flatman, William Bulman, Arthur Nicholson, Stanley Burbeck, Mr Winter and Mr Lewis.

St Columba's Church, East Howle. One of the many churches the Rev T.L. Lomax was responsible for during his long vicarage, until he retired in 1940. Built in 1894 by William Kay it was opened by the Dean of Durham and was to serve the needs of East Howle and Metal Bridge.

Lancelot Wilkinson, Vicar of St
Aidan's Church, Chilton.

Below: The interior of St Aidan's
Iron Church, Chilton. Built in 1904
it was destroyed by fire on 3rd
March 1928. The damage was
estimated at £4,000. The present
stone church was built in 1930,
credit for the rebuilding being due
to Vicar Lancelot Wilkinson.

Four Lane Ends, Chilton – St Aidan's Iron Church is recorded as having been built in 1877 but its early history is fairly obscure.

Parishioners standing outside the Sacred Heart RC Church Windlestone at the official opening and blessing by Bishop McCormick in 1948. The first parish priest was Father Jennings.

Kirk Merrington Church near Ferryhill. Of the many tombstones which you see behind the War Memorial, the most interesting perhaps is that of the three children of John Brass of Hill House Farm, between Merrington and Ferryhill who were killed in 1683 by a deranged farm servant Andrew Mills, who was afterwards executed and hung on a gibbet just South of the present Thinford Inn. The plot of land where the gibbet stood was thereafter called Gibbet Garth.

Church of St John, Kirk Merrington, drawn by R.W. Billings in 1846. The square tower is a landmark for miles around. In 1346 the roof of the tower was used as an observation post by the English during the battle of Nevilles Cross. It served the same purpose both during the First World War and the last war. The church which stands now, though of the same stones, is not the same building. In 1850 and 1851 it was almost entirely pulled down, rebuilt and enlarged using mostly the same stone, redressed and rearranged but with some alterations in the plan.

Let's say goodbye to the people of Ferryhill with this lovely postcard from the early 1900s showing a postman/porter carrying a briefcase which, when opened would unfold to reveal a number of views from the area. This example reads 'Greetings from Ferryhill'. Almost certainly the same postcard would have been used for several villages with the appropriate local views and the name changed on the briefcase.

Right: The images from the briefcase.